The Loophole

A Play

N. J. Warburton

[A Samuel French Acting Edition]

FOUNDED 1830

SAMUELFRENCH-LONDON.CO.UK
SAMUELFRENCH.COM

Copyright © 1992 by N. J. Warburton
All Rights Reserved

THE LOOPHOLE is fully protected under the copyright laws of the British Commonwealth, including Canada, the United States of America, and all other countries of the Copyright Union. All rights, including professional and amateur stage productions, recitation, lecturing, public reading, motion picture, radio broadcasting, television and the rights of translation into foreign languages are strictly reserved.

ISBN 978-0-573-04228-7

www.samuelfrench-london.co.uk

www.samuelfrench.com

FOR AMATEUR PRODUCTION ENQUIRIES

UNITED KINGDOM AND WORLD
EXCLUDING NORTH AMERICA
plays@SamuelFrench-London.co.uk
020 7255 4302/01

Each title is subject to availability from Samuel French,
depending upon country of performance.

CAUTION: Professional and amateur producers are hereby warned that THE LOOPHOLE is subject to a licensing fee. Publication of this play does not imply availability for performance. Both amateurs and professionals considering a production are strongly advised to apply to the appropriate agent before starting rehearsals, advertising, or booking a theatre. A licensing fee must be paid whether the title is presented for charity or gain and whether or not admission is charged.

The professional rights in this play are controlled by David Higham Associates Ltd, 7th Floor, Waverley House, 7–12 Noel Street, London W1F 8GQ.

No one shall make any changes in this title for the purpose of production. No part of this book may be reproduced, stored in a retrieval system, or transmitted in any form, by any means, now known or yet to be invented, including mechanical, electronic, photocopying, recording, videotaping, or otherwise, without the prior written permission of the publisher. No one shall upload this title, or part of this title, to any social media websites.

The right of N. J. Warburton to be identified as author of this work has been asserted by him in accordance with Section 77 of the Copyright, Designs and Patents Act 1988

THE LOOPHOLE

First presented at the Cambridge Drama Centre on August 15th, 1990 with the following cast of characters:

Mr Overall	Jonathan Broughton
Mr Perry	Jeremy Webb
Mr Cusp	Keith Craney
Mr Trumble	Peter Green

Directed by Kay Coe and Jenni Sinclair

The action takes place in the office of Mr Overall and in Mr Cusp's rooms in the prison. Both sets of rooms are to be found in a large castle
Time—the present

The Loophole won the Derrick Baldock Cup at the 1991 Welwyn Festival

CHARACTERS

Mr Overall, Junior Under Minister for Justice
Mr Perry, his assistant
Mr Cusp, a prison officer
Mr Trumble, a prison chaplain

THE LOOPHOLE

Scene 1

Overall's office. It is all rather grey

Perry is arranging papers as Overall sneaks in

Overall (*surprised*) Ah, Perry.
Perry Sir?
Overall I wasn't expecting you.
Perry No, sir? I'm usually here, sir.
Overall Well of course. Of course you are, Perry. I just thought you might be in the outer office.
Perry No, Mr Overall.
Overall No. Did you miss me?
Perry Sir?
Overall I was gone rather longer than I expected. I was just wondering...
Perry No, sir. I've been kept busy.
Overall Have you?
Perry The new chaplain started today. I've been slotting him into the filing system.
Overall Ah, Cardyke.
Perry No, sir. Trumble. Cardyke was considered too rigid if you

remember. I'm getting Cusp to show him round the cells.
Overall Ah. The famous social history of the castle.
Perry Yes, sir. Pigs in the yard.
Overall Of course. (*He sits*) Good. Good, good, good. The cogs still turn, then. As they should. (*Finding something on his desk*) What's this?
Perry PR 02.

Overall looks blank

Prison report form, sir.
Overall For me?
Perry I took the liberty of filling in your name and number, the date and...
Overall I don't do PR 02s. Do I?
Perry Well, not usually, no. However, it did occur to me...
Overall So why have I got one now? I mean, PR 02s. That's your province, isn't it, Perry?
Perry Is it, sir?
Overall Look, if you're feeling bad because I was late back from lunch...
Perry How long you spend over lunch is nothing to do with me...
Overall Yes but we both know the regulations. And I could've been back.
Perry You could, sir?
Overall Strictly between the two of us, I could, yes.
Perry But...?
Overall But I wasn't, I lingered, on purpose.
Perry Well, sir, I'm sure...
Overall No, Perry, I did it on purpose. Lingered. Expressly to be late. A case of Don't Walk on the Grass...
Perry Sir?
Overall Don't Walk on the Grass. You see a sign which forbids

The Loophole

you to put a foot on the grass and that's enough to make you want to do it.

Perry Is it, sir?

Overall Well of course. Don't you ever feel like putting your foot on forbidden grass, Perry?

Perry It's never occurred to me to do so, sir, no.

Overall An entirely pointless gesture, of course. I only do it when there's no one to see me. I deliberately linger over lunch after we've had a memo stressing the vital importance of getting Junior Under Minister bums back behind desks bang on time...

Perry I was wondering whether you'd forgotten Mr Jobbing's memo, sir.

Overall No, I hadn't forgotten it. In fact the memo is what made me want to do it. Give it five minutes, Overall, I told myself. After all you're a senior administrator up here...

Perry Five minutes, Mr Overall?

Overall Hmm. Just to make a point. A five minute act of defiance. And an extra doughnut. The idea of someone from the Ministry of Justice breaking regulations. On purpose. It was irresistible.

Perry But five minutes would have taken you to...

Overall To one fifty. Yes.

Perry And it's now...

Overall Half past two. Quite.

Perry So...

Overall I nodded off. Five minutes of sin and forty minutes of innocent sleep. Propped in a corner seat in the canteen. Which is why I was creeping somewhat when I came in.

Perry I see, sir.

Overall It's pathetic, isn't is? And then to nod off and come scuttling back here like a frightened rabbit.

Perry I wouldn't say that, sir.

Overall I hope you don't follow my example in this, Perry. I'd

take a dim view of it if you did.
Perry I wouldn't dream of being deliberately late.
Overall No, Perry. Of course not.
Perry I intend no criticism.
Overall I mean, if you're going to sin, go out and sin in a loud voice with a smile on your face. And don't come back with your heart beating because you only just managed to escape detection.
Perry I wouldn't quite say that either, sir.
Overall What?
Perry That you had escaped detection.
Overall What?
Perry Mr Jobbing was in, sir.
Overall The Under Minister? In here? While I was out?
Perry Yes, sir. I was surprised myself, sir.
Overall Oh God.
Perry It's my belief that he was following his memo round, sir.
Overall Checking, you mean. Oh God.
Perry Checking.
Overall This is life, Perry. Life in the raw. It isn't fair.
Perry (*beat*) I don't think you need worry too much.
Overall Not worry? You're talking about Jobbing, you realize. Bloodless Jobbing. He'll skin me for this. If I'm lucky, he'll skin me.
Perry Possibly not.
Overall (*looking up*) What?
Perry I was able to offer him an explanation. It seemed to satisfy him, sir.
Overall What explanation?
Perry I said you were engaged in research.
Overall I was?
Perry A spot check, sir. I said you'd gone down to the cells, sir. An impromptu visit, to check that all is as it should be.

Overall Did you?
Perry I took that liberty, sir.
Overall (*brightening*) While I was dozing over a doughnut?
Perry I know, sir. It sounds untruthful of me. But I didn't know about the doughnut, did I, sir?
Overall Well, no. No, of course not.
Perry I merely noted your absence and surmised that it must've been caused by business. Something like a spot check of the cells.
Overall Perry, you are a good and faithful servant. You will go far. I promise you, you will go far.
Perry I hope so, Mr Overall.
Overall Did he swallow it?
Perry Mr Jobbing seemed quite taken with the notion, sir. He thought it showed initiative.
Overall Did he?
Perry Yes, sir. I hope I haven't overstepped the mark.
Overall Far from it. Far from it. You showed considerable initiative yourself, Perry.
Perry Unfortunately my surmise has led to a slight complication.
Overall Has it?
Perry Mr Jobbing would like to see your report.
Overall Ah. Hence the PR 02?
Perry Yes, sir.
Overall Of course. Brilliant. Well, look, you usually do the PR 02s...
Perry I know, sir, but I think Mr Jobbing would like something from you. Something you might discuss with him. In your own hand, perhaps.
Overall Yes, I see. It would make sense. Perhaps you...
Perry Sir?
Overall Well, you do these PR 02s. If you just fill me in on what you see down there, and I jot down a few notes...

Perry I'm not sure that would do.
Overall No? Why not?
Perry It's true that I always complete the Prison Report forms but I have to confess that I do so without the aid of first-hand knowledge.
Overall Do you?
Perry I'm afraid so, sir. I make them up.
Overall Make them up, Perry? That's awful.
Perry It's a matter of expediency, sir. PR 02s are filled in and filed on time but I have reason to believe they are never actually read.
Overall Aren't they? Don't I read them?
Perry Do you, sir?
Overall Well, no. No, I don't. But someone must.
Perry I don't believe so, sir.
Overall I see. So what am I going to do?
Perry Well, sir, it did occur to me that you might actually visit the cells.
Overall Go down there, you mean?
Perry It might satisfy Mr Jobbing if you did.
Overall But... I mean, the cells...
Perry Sir?
Overall Well, they're full of criminals...
Perry Indeed they are, sir. But you would be accompanied by Cusp, I'm sure. And it might give you a useful insight into the broader aspects of the work.
Overall Might it?
Perry Contact with the criminal classes, sir.
Overall Hmm. I don't actually know where the cells are, Perry.
Perry I took the liberty of contacting Mr Cusp, sir.
Overall Did you?
Perry He knows where they are. He says he'll be more than happy to show you around.

Black-out

Scene 2

Cusp's room. Cusp and Trumble are taking tea and looking over the audience

Cusp This used to be a castle, sir. Were you aware of that?
Trumble Yes.
Cusp Many years ago the peasants used to gather down there in the yard during times of crisis. Tramp in from the fields, shut the gates. Fill the yard with straw and muck. You can no doubt imagine it.
Trumble Indeed.
Cusp Indeed, sir. Lucky peasants, eh? Better than having your head lopped off outside the castle walls, sir.
Trumble Barbaric times, Mr Cusp.
Cusp They used to let their pigs run free down there. So I've been told. I like to think of that.
Trumble I wonder what happened to them.
Cusp The pigs? It's my belief they moved indoors, sir.
Trumble Indoors?
Cusp Yes, sir. To take up administrative positions in the upper corridors. The Ministry of Justice.

Trumble smiles politely. They sit

Just through there is the long corridor, so called because of its length. Long corridor, long-term prisoners.
Trumble I see.
Cusp Coincidence actually, sir. They have to go somewhere. It starts this end with aggravated burglary and works its way up to the more heinous misdemeanours. Tax diddles and so on.
Trumble So on?

Cusp Murders. The valley of the shadow of death up there, it is. And I tread it twice a day. With scrambled egg and toast. It can clarify the mind, that kind of thing.
Trumble I'm sure it can.
Cusp I shouldn't fret, though. You'll get used to it. No doubt you'll have your rod and your staff to comfort you, sir. And, if not, I'll have mine. So no need to worry. You'll be quite safe.
Trumble I'll take your word for it.
Cusp We have one in for murder at the moment. 604, at the far end.
Trumble Yes, I've met 604.
Cusp He won't tell you much, though. 604 is one of the silent ones. You won't get much out of him.
Trumble Perhaps not.
Cusp Plenty will talk, sir. You'll have your work cut out shutting some of them up.
Trumble Assuming I want to.
Cusp Oh you will, sir. In the end.
Trumble I shall try to do what needs doing, Mr Cusp.
Cusp Of course, sir. You listen to them; they'll like that. You make a good listener, sir, I can tell that already.
Trumble There's more to it than listening.
Cusp I'm sure there is. Confession for one thing. They can be very keen on confession.
Trumble And prayer. There's always prayer.
Cusp That's right. Prayer. You pray for them too, sir. That'll put the sting into some of them.
Trumble As a matter of fact, 604 troubles me. He seemed ... I don't know... harmless.
Cusp Oh yes. He's harmlesss. Most of the time. A lamb of a man. I don't suppose he told you about the incident.
Trumble I didn't mention it. I don't feel I'm here to go over their crimes with them. Unless they want me to.

The Loophole

Cusp 604 wouldn't.
Trumble No. He's very quiet.
Cusp Which leaves little to talk about.
Trumble We didn't talk much. We played cards.
Cusp Cards? That's a novel approach.
Trumble It was just a way of being with him.
Cusp It's a very violent thing for a harmless man to have done, wouldn't you say, sir? Murder.
Trumble Well, I won't pretend I understand it.
Cusp If you do get anywhere, I'd be interested to know...
Trumble Mr Cusp, anything I discuss with prisoners...
Cusp Absolute confidence. Of course, sir. As it should be. (*Beat*) Did you get as far as 621, by any chance?
Trumble 621? No, I don't think so.
Cusp Oh, you'd remember 621, sir. A proper pervert. 621 is very good value. He's talkative, you see. Keen to confess.
Trumble I'm sure we all have things we could confess to...
Cusp Oh yes. Without doubt. But not quite with so much relish, perhaps. (*He drinks*) You wouldn't say he looked like a murderer, would you, sir?
Trumble 604? No. No, he looked, I don't know...
Cusp Incapable of it, sir. You're right. But it's my experience that murderers don't. Look capable, I mean.
Trumble The reason for that, Mr Cusp, is that we're all capable of the things these men are locked away for.
Cusp Really, sir? You think so? I can't imagine I'd have the time or the energy to get up to half the things 621 says he's done.
Trumble But murder, Mr Cusp. You'd be capable of murder, wouldn't you?
Cusp Well, possibly...
Trumble I think we all would. There's not that much that divides us from men like 604.
Cusp There's foot thick walls, sir. That's a start.

Trumble I didn't mean that.
Cusp No, sir. I know you didn't. We did have one bloke down here who looked like a murderer.
Trumble Really?
Cusp Only this morning, it was. Looked like sin in a suit, sir. Shifty, evil eyes. The lot.
Trumble What happened to him?
Cusp Nothing, sir. He was the Junior Under Minister, doing a spot check.
Trumble Mr Overall? He doesn't look evil.
Cusp You don't think so? Well, you're the expert.
Trumble No, I'm not, Mr Cusp. And I believe you've got it in for Mr Overall simply because he's from upstairs, the Ministry.
Cusp Yes, sir.
Trumble Well, that's hardly sufficient.
Cusp I wouldn't mind if they stayed where they belong. In the upper corridors. They usually do. Mr Overall's the exception to the rule in that respect.
Trumble Really?
Cusp Yes, sir. Him and Smiler are the only ones to show their face down here. Though not at the same time.
Trumble Smiler?
Cusp Mr Perry. We call him that out of the deepest affection, sir. I'm sure you understand.
Trumble Of course. I was under the impression that Mr Overall *didn't* visit.
Cusp Yes, sir. It's an impression that Mr Overall likes to cultivate. So I understand. We never see any of the others, though. Which is just the way I like it. Routine. Regular. The sun comes up, the scrambled eggs get made, the sun goes down. No one from upstairs visits. It's part of the routine, sir, no one coming to see us. The corridors ring with the absence of civil servants.

Trumble Hardly life in abundance, though, Mr Cusp.
Cusp I don't mind that, sir. I had life in abundance when I was twenty-two. And I'm still paying for it.
Trumble I don't know. Life should be abundant. Not lived on a tight rein all the time.
Cusp Maybe, sir. Althought 604 must be wishing he'd got a tight rein.
Trumble Has Mr Overall seen 604?
Cusp He has, sir, but I shouldn't be lulled into thinking that's significant. He's like all Junior Under Ministers.
Trumble Really?
Cusp Paperwork people, sir. Which means they achieve sod all.

Black-out

Scene 3

Overall's office. Perry feeds Overall papers which he signs absently

Overall The life of the place. Absolutely teeming with life. Each cell a chapter of fascinating stories. Very keen to speak, a lot of them down there. Very keen.
Perry I'm pleased to hear it. Plenty to put in Mr Jobbing's report.
Overall I don't think I could put much of it in a report, Perry. Not to Mr Jobbing, anyway. I shall restrict myself to observations about the food and the colour of the walls. All the same...
Perry One lives and learns.
Overall One certainly does. The confessions I heard down there. Do you know there was this little ferret of a man on one corridor. Caretaker in a nurses' home he was.
Perry 621?
Overall That's him. Absolute ferret of a man. All whinge and

cringe. Anyway, these poor angels were coming off the wards and shivering all night because he'd sold off their heating oil. Bloody mean thing to do, don't you think?
Perry Terrible, sir. To nurses of all people.
Overall Quite. Imagine them all coming on duty with chattering teeth. And frozen fingers. Bloody mean.
Perry I'm not surprised he wanted to confess.
Overall But that's just it, Perry. He was most indignant about being done for theft. "Everyone does that kind of thing" he said, "I shouldn't be locked up for that, your worship."
Perry He thought you could help him.
Overall No, no, he wanted to be locked up. He just thought he was in for the wrong thing.
Perry What was the right thing?
Overall You may well ask, Perry. (*Beat*) He insisted on telling me. "They weren't all cold, your worship," he said, "I kept a lot of them very warm. Personally."
Perry How did he do that, sir?
Overall Use your imagination, Perry. How do you think?
Perry (*after a moment's thought*) Really, sir?
Overall Absolutely. "I was their plaything," he said. "Some of the things I got up to with those nurses, your worship. If they put me away for that I'd have no complaints."
Perry Well, it could be arranged...
Overall I wouldn't go into it, Perry. We've got him locked away. Let's be thankful for that.
Perry It sounds to me more like wishful thinking than confession.
Overall Well, you could be right about that. He was certainly keen to fill me in on all the details.
Perry He was enjoying it.
Overall Undoubtedly. Mind you, I'm not altogether surprised. It's the sort of thing which, in weaker moments, I could enjoy

myself.
Perry I was meaning the confession, sir.
Overall So was I. There's something about confession which is, I don't know, satisfying.
Perry It clears the conscience, perhaps.
Overall Hmm. Quite compelling. I even found myself telling him about the doughnut.
Perry Well, sir, I'm glad the experience proved so rewarding.
Overall Rewarding. Yes. (*Beat*) Perry, what have we got on 604?
Perry 604?
Overall He never told me what he'd done. He was the only one I saw who didn't want to speak.
Perry I'm not surprised. 604 is in for murder, sir.
Overall Murder? Good grief. He seemed ... no more than a shadow.
Perry Well, murder it was, sir.
Overall So he'll be with us for some time, I suppose.
Perry No, sir. Not very much longer.
Overall No?
Perry They delayed sentencing him till the medical report was in.
Overall And is it in now?
Perry Yes. He's dim but normal according to the doctors.
Overall So what's happening?
Perry Sentence has just been passed, sir. 604 is to hang.
Overall Hang? But we...
Perry I know, sir. It'll be the first one under the reinstated legislation. But so it has been decreed.
Overall Has it? I mean, it's certain, is it?
Perry It is now, sir. You've just signed the documentation.

Perry takes the paper Overall has just signed and leaves

Black-out

Scene 4

Overall's office. Overall picks up a paper dart from his desk and flies it. It lands somewhere near Trumble as he enters

Overall Ah, Chaplain. Good of you to come.
Trumble You sent for me.
Overall Well, yes. A message has reached its destination for once. You know, sometimes I send a message by one of those creeps in the outer office and nothing comes of it, absolutely nothing, and I forget I sent it in the first place.
Trumble I see.
Overall And the matter just seems to drift away. Sometimes it solves itself and, well...
Trumble Sometimes not.
Overall Quite. By the way, when I refer to the creeps I wouldn't want you to think I include Perry amongst them.
Trumble Of course not, sir.
Overall Although he is. A creep of the first water, as a matter of fact. I just wouldn't want you to think I was meaning him. Or to say so.
Trumble Your secret is safe with me, Mr Overall.
Overall Oh, good. I'm sure it is.
Trumble (*after a slight pause*) Is there something I can do, sir?
Overall Ah, yes. About your prison work.
Trumble Sir?
Overall I've been digging into a few files up here and it seems to me that, as prison chaplain, it's your job to attend to any little spiritual matter the prisoners may have, give communion where it's asked for. That kind of thing.
Trumble Yes, sir.
Overall What's not quite clear is who you work for.

The Loophole

Trumble I serve the church, sir.
Overall Yes, of course. Of course you serve the church. We all do, in our own way, I suppose. We are, after all, a Christian country, aren't we? Officially. But I wasn't exactly meaning that. I was wondering who paid you.
Trumble Who pays? Well, I suppose you do. At least for the prison work.
Overall Yes, that's what I thought.
Trumble Is this leading up to anything? Because I could be...
Overall There's no need to sound defensive, Mr Trumble. I'm just trying to clarify things. So, you work for the church, and we, that is the state, pay you?
Trumble Yes. The church is an established part...
Overall Yes, yes, I know. Your duty is to whom exactly?
Trumble To God.
Overall Apart from Him, I mean.
Trumble Well... to the prisoners.
Overall You're sure?
Trumble There's nothing on paper but that's the way I see it, yes.
Overall Good. That's the way I'd see it too, if I were a priest.
Trumble I see. Will that be all?
Overall Well, yes, I suppose so. Except... I was just wondering about 604.
Trumble He's a prisoner so I help him where I can.
Overall By playing cards? According to Cusp.
Trumble You've seen him yourself, Mr Overall. He doesn't want to talk.
Overall Yes but cards. Is this some tangential approach to spirituality, Trumble? Some sort of unorthodox dash round the blind side of the scrum as it were?
Trumble I'm afraid I don't know what else to do. (*Sharply*) He's waiting to be executed.
Overall Yes, I know. I've been briefed by Perry.

Trumble I did try to talk about spiritual matters but he wasn't interested. It seemed heartless to abandon him for that reason.
Overall Oh, I quite agree.
Trumble I think he appreciates the contact—just being with another person for a few moments—before he dies.
Overall So the cards fill a void?
Trumble I suppose they do. I know it sounds trivial. As if I'm wasting state time...
Overall Oh, not at all.
Trumble ...but we weren't getting anywhere when I mentioned God. It's easier to play cards.
Overall How clever of you.
Trumble It's not clever at all. I don't want to trap him or make him confess. It doesn't matter to me what he's done.
Overall Of course. But the fact remains...
Trumble Murder.
Overall Indeed.
Trumble And he has to die.
Overall Ah.
Trumble Ah?
Overall Yes, ah.
Trumble I'm sorry, I don't understand.
Overall I must be careful what I say. (*He nods towards the outer office*) Creep, creep, if you see what I mean. (*Pause*) Do you know how I came to be Under Minister for Justice?
Trumble I've no idea. By creeping yourself?
Overall I don't know. Perhaps I did, although I wasn't aware I was doing it. Anyway I didn't mean that.
Trumble How, then?
Overall I have a particular talent.
Trumble Really?
Overall For loopholes.
Trumble (*unimpressed*) Fascinating.

The Loophole 17

Overall I can spot a loophole in a piece of proposed legislation, give it a tweak and lo, all becomes smooth again. *(Pause)* You don't seem impressed.
Trumble Well, in the context of a man's life, it seems irrelevant to me. Not to say rather boring. Sorry.
Overall Not at all. It is boring to most people. Rather a timid kind of talent, if you see what I mean.
Trumble Mr Overall, you're still going to execute 604, aren't you?
Overall Not me personally, God forbid.
Trumble It'll be your signature, though won't it?
Overall It takes more than one signature for a thing like that. Including that of Mr Jobbing himself.
Trumble That's not much comfort, I'm afraid. How long has he got?
Overall Well, I can't really say.
Trumble He's going to die, Mr Overall. Isn't he entitled to know when?
Overall Yes, I would've thought so. But I'm not just being awkward. I can't say because I don't know.
Trumble Then perhaps you should find out.
Overall I could push the matter, I suppose, yes.
Trumble If it's not too much trouble, you mean.
Overall No, it's not that. If I go prying into executioners' timetables and wot-not, someone somewhere is going to fix a date and...
Trumble Yes?
Overall Well, then they'll have to go through with it, won't they?
Trumble I see.
Overall If we don't stir things up, it could give 604 a bit of breathing space. If that's not too unfortunate a way of putting it.
Trumble Why are you telling me this? I thought it was your job to push these things through.

Overall It's simple. I met 604. Quite by chance. And when I discovered... these recent developments...
Trumble That he's going to die.
Overall Yes. Well, to tell you the truth, I didn't like it.
Trumble I can appreciate that. I don't think 604 likes it very much.
Overall He's going to die and I know about it and I can't unknow it.
Trumble So, what are you going to do about it?
Overall Ah.
Trumble Ah? What's that supposed to mean?
Overall It means that I think I've discovered one of my loopholes. It's forty years since we had a hanging so you won't have attended a condemned man before, will you?
Trumble No. Thank God.
Overall Then perhaps you are not acquainted with the procedure?
Trumble Procedure? For a prison chaplain. I didn't know there was a procedure.
Overall Of course, there are procedures for everything. There are certain procedures regarding a condemned person's progress to the gallows. And from it, for that matter. There is a trial...
Trumble A trial!
Overall (*sighing*) There is a trial of sorts, a sentence, a spell in solitary and so on. There is also provision made for the condemned man's soul. Which brings us to you. You must provide the state with documentation concerning the prisoner's spiritual state.
Trumble So I have to sign something as well?
Overall You see. You didn't know that, did you?
Trumble No one told me.
Overall No. It's one of those little procedures which has lapsed into a sort of formality.

The Loophole

Trumble What do you mean by 'a sort of formality'?
Overall Well, in years gone by someone upstairs always signed the document.
Trumble A civil servant?
Overall Extremely civil if it's done in the outer office.
Trumble That's ridiculous.
Overall Is it any more ridiculous for a civil servant than a priest? I don't know.
Trumble What's all this leading to?
Overall This peculiar document is supposed to tell us that the prisoner has been accepted into the Church. Cleared for take-off, you might say. Has 604 been accepted into the Church, Trumble?
Trumble I haven't got as far as asking.
Overall Splendid.
Trumble Splendid?
Overall For our purposes, yes. Are you about to accept the prisoner into the Church?
Trumble Well, I would, of course. But not simply to tie up odd bits of red-tape. That's not what the Church is for.
Overall I was rather hoping you'd take that approach.
Trumble Look, I still don't see what this...
Overall My dear Trumble, if the document is not signed then the correct procedure has broken down. We can't have our execution.
Trumble We can't?
Overall No. And you won't sign, will you?
Trumble (*after a pause*) Are you really telling me that 604's life depends on my signature?
Overall Yes. Exactly.
Trumble But if it's been done in the past, it can be done again. Any of them out there. Perry...
Overall Please, keep your voice down.

Trumble Perry would do it like a shot. And pull the lever.
Overall He wouldn't.
Trumble Oh yes he would. It's in his creed. Laws before life.
Overall I mean he wouldn't pull the lever because he wouldn't be allowed to. Not without signing first. That would be murder.
Trumble But if he signed and then pulled the lever, that wouldn't be murder?
Overall No. That would be execution. At least, it would if he was qualified.
Trumble You have to be qualified?
Overall Of course. You can't expect anyone to wander in off the street and execute people.
Trumble (*becoming irate*) How do you become qualified for a job like that?
Overall I don't now. You'd have to ask Perry.
Trumble Evening classes?
Overall I've really no idea.
Trumble Because 604 could do with something to occupy his mind. It might make a change from cards.
Overall I feel we're straying from the point somewhat.
Trumble Maybe he could learn how to dispatch himself. Even cheaper than getting Perry to do it. The self-executing prisoner. Like a self-basting turkey.
Overall Please, Mr Trumble...
Trumble I've often wondered how they get them to do it. I mean, how do you baste yourself when you've been plucked and you've got your feet tucked up your own backside?
Overall Yes, well, I shouldn't worry about that, if I were you. We only go in for conventional executions and I'm doing my best to see that we won't even do that.
Trumble Because you can't go ahead without my signature?
Overall Yes. You're not qualified to execute people but you *are* qualified to sign the proper document. And I am qualified to

make sure that no other signature will be accepted. That's the loophole.

Black-out

Scene 5

Cusp's room. Cusp is about to light up his pipe when Perry enters with a clipboard. Cusp hurriedly puts the pipe away and stands

Perry Something troubling you, Cusp?
Cusp No, sir. I just wasn't expecting...
Perry Mr Overall is busy elsewhere. (*Glancing at the clipboard*) You are required to record the prisoner's height.
Cusp Done, sir. Although he didn't know why I was doing it.
Perry You are required to weigh him.
Cusp Sir.
Perry To make allowances for his age and physique. To assess the strength of his neck.
Cusp Yes, sir. He has a good neck, sir.
Perry A strong neck, Cusp?
Cusp Hard to say, sir. Do you want me to devise a test? I could, perhaps, keep him in ignorance as to its purpose. He's not a difficult man to fool.
Perry I don't think that will be necessary.
Cusp Or I could, of course, tell him why I want to test his neck.
Perry There's no need.
Cusp But it wouldn't bother you if I did, Mr Perry, would it?
Perry No it wouldn't bother me, Cusp. Would it bother you?
Cusp Would it matter to the Ministry if it did, Mr Perry?
Perry (*beat*) If it mattered to the Ministry, Cusp, would you do anything about it?
Cusp (*looking away*) I don't know, sir.

Perry Perhaps you don't need to know. I certainly don't need you to know.

Cusp Fair enough, Mr Perry. I wouldn't want to get ideals above my station.

Perry There is a Ministry Standard Table of Drops. (*He hands him a pen*) The intention is to see that the break is clean.

Cusp I see. Clean, sir.

Perry I'm assuming you haven't done this kind of thing before.

Cusp No, sir.

Perry We need a clean break. Not for your sake or mine but for 604's. The calculation is a simple one. One thousand two hundred and sixty foot-pounds divided by the prisoner's weight in pounds. Which will give you the correct drop.

Cusp If required.

Perry If required?

Cusp The Chaplain hasn't signed him in yet, Mr Perry.

Perry No. But he will, I'm sure. He can't dither indefinitely.

Cusp Dither, sir? I don't know that it's dithering.

Perry If it's not dithering it's a deliberate abuse of the law. You're not suggesting that Mr Trumble would abuse the law, are you, Mr Cusp?

Cusp I'm only wondering why we're going through the drill when we don't know that we'll need it.

Perry We're going through the drill because the law requires us to. And Mr Jobbing is quite rightly insistent that, since we are sticking so doggedly to the law in this case, we stick to it in every detail.

Cusp I see, sir.

Perry So. You are to test the trap. A sandbag weighing the same as the prisoner. Drop it several times.

Cusp Sir.

Perry And let it hang overnight.

Cusp To make sure, sir?

The Loophole

Perry To make sure?
Cusp That it's dead.
Perry To remove the possibility of the rope stretching, Cusp. A humanitarian measure.
Cusp Really?
Perry To avoid whiplash.
Cusp Of course, sir. And this will be in the yard, will it, sir?
Perry In the yard. Of course.
Cusp Where the prisoner can see.
Perry That's right. Where the prisoner can see.
Cusp I understood that it was the custom to keep such preparations out of sight, Mr Perry. Of the prisoner.
Perry Really?
Cusp Mr Overall mentioned as much.
Perry Custom is not law, Mr Cusp.
Cusp No, sir.
Perry Thank you for your attention, Mr Cusp.
Cusp That's all right, sir.

Perry exits

Perhaps I can do the same for you one day.

Black-out

Scene 6

Overall's office. Trumble leans against the filing cabinet deep in thought

Overall It's working, Mr Trumble. I do believe it's working.
Trumble I'm not sure, sir. I find myself in a most peculiar position.

Overall You do?
Trumble It is my duty as Chaplain to talk to 604 about God and yet I know that's the one subject I mustn't mention.
Overall I see. He's touchy about it, is he?
Trumble It isn't that. I must seek to draw him into the comfort of the Church, but if I succeed he dies.
Overall But you won't succeed, will you?
Trumble I don't know.
Overall I don't think you will. 604 isn't interested in God.
Trumble He doesn't understand the God I talk about. He has in mind a picture book God. A kind old man who looks after animals.
Overall You can let him think that, can't you?
Trumble It's not as simple as that, though.
Overall Oh dear, isn't it?
Trumble No. What matters is how hard do I try?
Overall For the sake of the Church?
Trumble No, for the sake of the prisoner.
Overall (*considering*) Well, I should've thought you could go at three-quarters throttle and still stay the right side of an execution.
Trumble But I can't do that!
Overall I'm sure he won't succumb...
Trumble That's not the point. Am I trying to save his soul, regardless of his bodily death, or am I ever so slightly back-pedalling in order to keep him alive?
Overall Well, you're the only one who can answer that.
Trumble That's my problem. I don't know. I honestly don't know what I'm doing. Or why.
Overall Hmm. A loophole in the loophole, you might say.
Trumble Even looking at it from his point of view there's a problem.
Overall Is there?

The Loophole

Trumble The prisoner is a simple man. He doesn't say much but he does care. He cares about what happened.
Overall I should think so.
Trumble About the people involved. He's cut to the soul to think of them suffering.
Overall That seems reasonable enough, doesn't it?
Trumble Of course it's reasonable. If it's genuine it also approaches the second great commandment.
Overall Does it?
Trumble 'Love your neighbour as yourself.' Which would put him half way there.
Overall But I thought there were ten commandments. That still leaves him nine short.
Trumble Our Lord gave us two. All others spring from those.
Overall Really? Just the two?
Trumble Two are quite enough. If you take them seriously.
Overall And no loopholes?
Trumble It doesn't work like that. They're commandments not regulations. (*Pause*) I've turned this over and over in my mind. If the prisoner can accept them, even at the simplest level, the Church should accept him. And I would have to say so.
Overall Hmm. Tricky.
Trumble Which would mean me signing his death warrant.
Overall Just jog my memory about the other commandment, will you?
Trumble 'You shall love the Lord your God with all your heart and with all your soul and with all your strength.'
Overall Yes, well, we're on safer ground there, surely. That sounds well beyond 604's reach to me.
Trumble You shouldn't underestimate him, Mr Overall. Or God for that matter.
Overall Suppose you refused to sign?
Trumble Refusal to sign would be a denial of my own beliefs.

Overall Oh, I don't think anyone would hold you to that.
Trumble I would.
Overall (*sighing*) This is partly my fault, isn't it?
Trumble No, Mr Overall, I'm not blaming you.
Overall But we wouldn't be facing this problem without the loophole.
Trumble True, but the prisoner would be already dead.
Overall Hmm. You couldn't go back to the cards for while, could you?

Black-out

Scene 7

Overall's office. Overall finds Perry arranging papers etc. He tosses more paper in front of him

Overall More paperwork. Hot from Jobbing's out-tray.
Perry You've seen Mr Jobbing, sir?
Overall I have. It's one of the irksome burdens of office, Perry. Occasional encounters with Bloodless Jobbing.
Perry And did he have ... anything of interest to impart, Mr Overall?
Overall Like what?
Perry Oh, I don't know. Of a general nature, perhaps.
Overall Not that I noticed. I don't think he goes in for things of interest, does he?
Perry No, sir?
Overall Well, I've consistently failed to interest him over the years but perhaps that's just me. I did try. I was telling him about the antics of our friend from the nurses' hostel.
Perry Really, sir?
Overall Yes. To add a little spice to his life.

The Loophole

Perry But he didn't respond?
Overall No. It just seemed to confuse him. And the only result was, well, more paperwork.
Perry Quite. It has increased dramatically in the past few weeks, sir.
Overall (*sitting*) That's in the nature of paperwork.
Perry But most of this concerns the execution, sir. Or rather, the non-execution.
Overall Ah.
Perry And, if the hanging went ahead, I believe the bottle-neck would clear.
Overall As I see it, we're merely sticking to what the law actually says.
Perry The letter, not the spirit.
Overall The letter of the law embodies the spirit. That's why it's so bloody complicated. It's why I exist, Perry. To see that the law is carried out. To the letter.
Perry I'm not sure, Mr Overall. That's well and good if the law is perfect. But it isn't, is it?
Overall Then we must endeavour to perfect it.
Perry And meanwhile we have to suffer its injustices.
Overall In general, perhaps, yes. In this case, though, I can't see that the law is supporting any particular injustice.
Perry Don't you, sir?
Overall No, to be frank. In this case the law is turning out to be rather a good thing.
Perry As you see it. At the moment.
Overall At the moment?
Perry Yes, sir. Things change.
Overall Things? What things?
Perry It's only hearsay, sir.
Overall Well, I haven't heard.
Perry It seems that 604 could, technically, be accepted into the Church.

Overall What?
Perry Without actually knowing it, sir. Quite innocently, in fact.
Overall You mean, Trumble might sign?
Perry No...
Overall He can't sign without consulting 604.
Perry Apparently he could, sir. If he felt within his heart, that 604 is a true Christian.
Overall You can't go around declaring people to be Christians. You can't do that.
Perry The law doesn't say you can't. And, as you said yourself, the law...
Overall Yes, I know what I said.
Perry It's been done before, Mr Overall. In Africa and South America.
Overall But it doesn't make sense. I mean you could declare the Buddha a Christian, couldn't you? Half an hour with a pile of forms and a fountain pen and the archbishop could convert the world.
Perry I don't think he'd be prepared to do that.
Overall Then why pick on 604?
Perry *(facing the front)* Mr Trumble is experiencing considerable anguish over the case, sir. Mr Jobbing has become concerned about his health.

Cusp backs on, trying to prevent Trumble entering

Overall holds up a hand to quieten them

Overall Really? Since when has Jobbing concerned himself with anyone's health?
Perry Since I broached the subject with him, Mr Overall.
Overall You did?
Perry Trumble seemed to be under a great deal of stress. I was

quite worried for him.
Overall Were you?
Perry Yes. I could see the turmoil he was in. It occurred to me that he could be saved from that.
Trumble (*stepping forward*) That's very thoughtful of you, Perry.
Perry Mr Trumble...
Cusp Sorry, Mr Perry. He said he was entitled to come up here.
Trumble Well of course.
Perry All right, Cusp. Just wait there.
Trumble Just as I'm entitled to be in some kind of turmoil.
Perry I was thinking of...
Trumble I certainly don't want to be saved from it by you.
Overall He's right, Perry. You can't take over his conscience for him.
Perry It seemed to me that Mr Trumble's conscience was taking over our duty.
Overall Oh? Does it matter how it seemed to you?
Perry Mr Jobbing thought so.
Overall This seems rather more than hearsay to me. (*To Trumble*) I think there's something he's not telling me, Mr Trumble.
Perry But I am telling you, Mr Overall. That's what I'm doing now.
Overall And what are you telling me? Because, at the moment, it's failing to penetrate.
Trumble What he's telling you, I think, is that I've been replaced.
Overall What?
Trumble That's right, isn't it, Perry?
Perry For reasons of health. As I said.
Trumble Well. Here I stand. (*He makes a sudden grab at Perry's collar*) I feel fit enough.
Cusp (*intervening*) Now now, sir.

Overall Mr Trumble, please.

Perry (*detaching himself*) I'm not talking about physical health...

Trumble I see, I'm cracking up, am I?

Cusp (*to Perry*) Would you like me to see him out, sir?

Overall Just a minute, Cusp. I want to get this straight. Mr Trumble has been replaced?

Cusp He has.

Overall Who by?

Perry By Mr Jobbing.

Overall I mean, who is to be the new chaplain?

Perry I see. Mr Cardyke, sir.

Overall Of course. The rigid Mr Cardyke. Mr Trumble, I can assure you this was not my doing.

Trumble Obviously.

Overall But we'll work something out. You can't be removed without my say so.

Trumble Can't I?

Overall Of course not. It would be most... irregular.

Trumble Would be? Has been, Mr Overall. (*A look at Cusp*) I have been irregularly excluded from the cells.

Cusp I welcomed you with open arms, sir. When it was official.

Overall (*sorting through papers*) You can't have been excluded.

Cusp Now that Mr Cardyke has started, I have to curb my natural hospitality.

Overall Already started? Perry, is this true?

Perry The prisoners shouldn't be denied access to a chaplain.

Trumble Especially the ones who are due to hang.

Overall The prisoners had access to a chaplain.

Perry They had access to a man who refused them proper spiritual guidance.

Overall How would you know about that?

Perry Cusp?

The Loophole 31

Cusp He played cards, sir. That's all I know.
Trumble Cards! I refused to sign your document, you mean.
Overall And Cardyke will sign, I suppose.
Perry He has seen 604.
Cusp He tells me he was impressed by 604's expressions of remorse.
Overall Will he sign?
Trumble He has signed.
Cusp Everything's been done most correctly, Mr Overall. I think you'll be pleased.
Overall Really? You think so?
Cusp I'll be disappointed if you're not, sir. All is in readiness. The mark on the trap so we know where to stand him. A drink to calm his nerves. The hood. The strap to go round his legs.
Overall For God's sake, Perry.
Perry (*consulting a form on the desk*) Yes. Nine o'clock next Monday morning. So it would appear.
Cusp Very shortly after nine, yes, sir.
Overall Without my signature?
Perry (*consulting the form*) Without your signature.
Overall This is monstrous. Why didn't I know about this?
Perry It wasn't deemed necessary.
Overall Oh really? And who didn't deem it necessary? Jobbing?
Perry As a matter of fact, sir, I didn't. Although Mr Jobbing was in agreement with me.
Overall (*pause*) Well. How very... friendly.
Perry He was of the opinion that the law was not being properly used in this case.
Overall You don't use the law, Perry! The law is for our protection. Not for our use.
Perry Really? Haven't you been using the law for your own ends?
Overall No. I've been applying the law as it exists. Just trying to

do a little good. Within the confines of the law.
Trumble Well maybe that's where we went wrong.
Cusp You have to stick to the rules, sir. 604 ought to know that.
Perry After all, they're the State's laws. And the State is the people.
Overall Balls, Mr Perry. Absolute balls.
Perry I would've thought it was absolute balls to set yourself above the state. A decent Junior Under Minister should never do that.
Overall A decent...
Perry Which you have ceased to be.
Overall It's not your job to make judgements about my performance, Perry.
Perry Well, it used not to be.
Overall It still isn't, man!
Perry I'm sure Mr Jobbing would have stopped me if he didn't like what I was saying.
Overall (*quietly*) You creep. You bloody little creep.
Perry Yes, sir. We're all creeps in the outer office, aren't we, sir?
Overall (*jumping up*) I'm going to see Jobbing about this...
Perry Of course. As long as you go through the proper channels.
Overall What do you mean by that?
Perry Put in an application to the Junior Under Minister. (*Gathering up his papers*) In writing.
Overall To the...
Perry And I'll consider it.

Perry smiles and leaves

Overall sits at the desk. Pause

Cusp As you say, sir. A bloody little creep.
Overall Which won't stop you working for him, I suppose, Cusp.

The Loophole

Cusp Oh no, sir. I didn't let the personal failings of the upper corridors get in the way when you were in charge, Mr Overall. I shan't now.

Cusp exits with a pleasant smile

Overall Well, at least we know where we stand with a man like Cusp, Mr Trumble.
Trumble As if it matters any more.
Overall Tell me, did you ever believe that a signature would've made any real difference?
Trumble I believed it was keeping a man alive. Which is a considerable difference really.
Overall Yes but, serious as that was, it was still a kind of formality. It didn't change the man himself. Not just by signing a piece of paper.
Trumble If you're saying we've lost our jobs but kept our dignity...
Overall No, I'm not. At least, not exactly.
Trumble Because that's a poor thing to set against a man's life.
Overall Quite so. What I really mean is that what matters is what a man thinks and feels, not what the law says about him.
Trumble A man is about to die, Mr Overall. I'd say that matters too.
Overall But I'm not talking about the prisoner.
Trumble You're not?
Overall No. I'm talking about excommunication.
Trumble Excommunication?
Overall Or defrocking. Is that what you call it? Defrocking? It always sounded so sordid.
Trumble Perry wants me out of the way. I don't think he's bothered about...
Overall Oh, I'm not talking about you either, Mr Trumble. I'm

talking about your successor.
Trumble Cardyke?
Overall Yes, I'm worried about what Cardyke thinks and feels. His soul, if you like.
Trumble You're worried about Cardyke's soul?
Overall As far as I understand it. In a lay kind of way. I mean, if poor old Cardyke suddenly finds himself quite unfairly defrocked, he will survive with his integrity intact, won't he?
Trumble But Cardyke hasn't done anything.
Overall No. Of course not. Not as far as I know.
Trumble So?
Overall (*beat*) It had to be concocted.
Trumble Concocted?
Overall It was talking to 621 that gave me the idea. All those naughty goings-on with nurses. I had a word with Jobbing who somehow got the impression that I was talking about Cardyke.
Trumble You mean to say you've framed Cardyke?
Overall Yes, I suppose so. Awful, isn't it? Maybe it's my soul I ought to be worrying about. All the same, it seems to have worked.
Trumble So Cardyke's signature won't count?
Overall No. Jobbing's a great man for pulling strings in high places. And infinitely persuadable, as you can tell from Perry's attempted coup.
Trumble And we're back where we were?
Overall For the time being.
Trumble I see. You knew what Perry was up to all along?
Overall Yes. Perry is a babe in arms when it comes to this sort of manipulation.
Trumble Then why didn't you say so just now?
Overall Oh, I rather enjoyed seeing him dig his own pit. He's teetering on the edge of it at the moment, Mr Trumble, but he will fall in, believe me.
Trumble So. The game goes on.

Overall It does for the moment. We find ourselves in extra time, at it were.
Trumble An endless queue of prison chaplains, alternately signing and refusing to sign.
Overall Well, I hope not. Once Perry's gone.
Trumble A matter of laws and loopholes and...
Overall And what men believe, I suppose.
Trumble Quite. And, in the meantime...

Overall takes a doughnut from the drawer in his desk

Overall In the meantime, Mr Trumble, as you say, the game goes on.

He divides the doughnut and offers half to Trumble. The Lights fade, music plays. Black-out

FURNITURE AND PROPERTY LIST

Scene 1

Overall's office
On stage: Desk. *On it*: papers
              Filing cabinet
              Chairs

Scene 2

Cusp's room
On stage: General furniture
Personal: **Cusp and Trumble**: cups of tea

Scene 3

On stage: As Scene 1
Personal: **Perry**: papers
              Overall: pen

Scene 4

On stage: As Scene 1
Personal: **Overall**: paper dart

Scene 5

On stage: As Scene 2
Personal: **Cusp**: pipe and lighter
              Perry: clipboard

Scene 6

On stage: As Scene 1

Scene 7

On stage: As Scene 1
Set: Doughnut in desk drawer
Personal: **Perry**: papers
Overall: papers

LIGHTING PLOT

Property fittings required: nil
2 interior settings

SCENE 1

To open: general interior lighting on Overall's office
Cue 1 **Perry:** "...show you around." (Page 6)
Black-out

SCENE 2

To open: general interior lighting on Cusp's room
Cue 2 **Cusp:** "... sod all." (Page 11)
Black-out

SCENE 3

To open: general interior lighting on Overall's office
Cue 3 **Perry:** "... the documentation." (Page 13)
Black-out

SCENE 4

To open: general interior lighting on Overall's office
Cue 4 **Overall:** "... the loophole." (Page 21)
Black-out

SCENE 5

To open: general interior lighting on Cusp's room
Cue 5 **Cusp:** "... you one day." (Page 23)
Black-out

Scene 6
To open: general interior lighting on Overall's office
Cue 6   **Overall**: "...could you?"   (Page 26)
    Black-out

Scene 7
To open: general interior lighting on Overall's office
Cue 7   **Overall**: "...game goes on."   (Page 35)
    Black-out

EFFECTS PLOT

Cue 1 As the Lights fade (Page 35)
Music

www.ingramcontent.com/pod-product-compliance
Lightning Source LLC
Chambersburg PA
CBHW070453050426
42450CB00012B/3251